Christmas
On The Move
Out West

Matthew Gonder

...for those who created these beautiful
and unforgettable memories with me.

TABLE OF CONTENTS
(The Twelve Days of Christmas)

ACKNOWLEDGMENTS

I wish to thank my brothers Mark and John Gonder, for their patience and cooperation in answering my constant queries via telephone and email to help me clarify certain facts in these true stories, Carroll Saint Paul for graciously cleaning up my document and for making sure that the images in my mind and heart were clearly depicted on the page to share with others, and Dan Benesch for capturing the essence of this story in his incredible book cover. But most of all, I owe this endeavor entirely to my wife, Pamela Gonder, who inspired and encouraged me to sit down and write this story the moment I recounted it to her.

1. CHUMP CHANGE

"Sticks and stones" as the saying goes. Go ahead and call me a nostalgic baby boomer if you like. I can take it, because whatever label you choose floats away meaninglessly as my mind serenely drifts back to early dawn on December 1, 1968, to a slightly slanted, turn-of-the-century home nestled in the Overlook neighborhood on Emerson Street in Portland, Oregon. Today, in 2012, Overlook has become a trendy place to live. Back then it was a weatherworn area not far from the wrong side of the railroad tracks and the Willamette River, where middle-class families made do behind doors that were never locked.

At our house, everyone was asleep. Well, almost. Upstairs, my little sisters Monica and Marguerite were slumbering away in their room, and I'm sure the whole neighborhood could hear Dad saw logs in his room across the hall. Downstairs, Aunt Mary, Dad's sister, was probably passed out in what was at one time the dining room, but had become her bedroom since we moved in over a year ago. I'm guessing she was 'probably' passed out because we hadn't seen much of her that week. She was on one of her drinking binges and would hole up, making a quick pass through the house from time to time if she needed another bottle or to use the bathroom.

The walls creaked and groaned rhythmically as the house slowly sank to its grave, but the noises had become so commonplace that no one really heard them anymore. In our bedroom upstairs, my big brothers Mark and John were pulling on whatever clothes they had tossed within arm's reach near their bunk beds the night before. John, shivering, peered out the window into the back yard, then turned around to face Mark, buttoning his shirt in a sleepy daze.

"We're gonna get wet today, Mark."

John pointed out the window. Mark looked and then shook his head.

"Oh Man."

Nodding their heads in unison, Mark bent over my lower bunk bed, speaking in a loud whisper.

"Hey, Matt."

"Mmm?"

"Matt, wake up, it's snowing."

"What?"

"C'mon, get up. Look out the window. I'm not kiddin'."

John grinned and added his two cents to the charade.

"It's neat, Matt. Check it out."

Snow was a rarity in the Pacific Northwest, where cold rains are usually par for the winter course, but I had experienced mounds of it when we lived in Spokane. My brothers knew I couldn't forget all the fun we had, so they succeeded in stirring my curiosity. I sat up, rubbing my eyes.

"Really?"

I crawled out of my bunk bed, wrapped my blanket around my body and ambled over to wipe my clenched fist on the foggy window. Mark was lying. I turned and glared at my brothers as they retrieved unmatched socks from the floor, smelling each one to choose the cleanest among the dirty that lay strewn amidst the broken toys and junk all over the bedroom.

"That's rain, not snow," I said, adding, "and I'm not helping you guys."

"You'll get twenty-five cents."

Big deal. That was the normal fee. I didn't budge. Mark sweetened the offer.

"And I'll buy ya a Slurpee if you do."

Slurpees were THE cool drink back then, but before caving in so quickly, I took Mark's offer as an invitation for some hard bargaining.

"A Slurpee AND a bag of Doritos."

We all were big fans of those spicy corn chips invented in the mid-60's and treated ourselves as often as we could to the popular junk food, but then John threw a wrench into my wheel.

"God, Matt. It's Sunday and it's rainin'. Don't be so greedy. It's your fault we got so many to deliver anyway, ya wimp."

Well, I couldn't argue there. Originally, Mark had approximately 80 Oregonians to deliver and John had 60, until I took a route that only lasted a couple of weeks since I was a fifth grade scaredy-cat, afraid of venturing out alone into unknown neighborhoods in the dark, and of the big barking dogs that chased me into the street. When I quit, Mr. Spiedel, the route manager, broke protocol and allowed Mark and John to take over and split my route, because the Gonder boys were known for always delivering their papers, come hell or high water. On days when weather conditions rendered the job uncomfortable, we still got the job done. We might not finish the task until noon but we did it and were known for our reliability. So, thanks to my lack of courage, Mark's route expanded to 127 papers and John's to 105. To them it seemed only fair that I be enlisted to help out when needed 'after all they were doing for me', which was often enough for the executive level salary of twenty-five cents per day, and that's why I include myself when I say "we" got the job done.

Yes, at our house, we were all slaves to the Oregonian to some extent. Dad helped out with his car on a rare occasion, and it wasn't an uncommon sight to see Monica and Marguerite out there on weekends dragging the red wagon piled high with newspapers in exchange for anywhere from ten to twenty cents each, depending on how hard they bartered. Our sisters may have been in the fourth and third grades, respectively, but they could have given master classes on the art of negotiation despite their tender ages. Any Gonder worth his salt could have done the same. Today, you have to be over eighteen and own your own car to acquire an Oregonian paper route. My four siblings and I were of the ages between eight and twelve with bikes and a wagon, which shows you how times have changed. But I wasn't going to let my big brothers exploit me that easy for peanuts. Even though I was nothing more than cheap child labor, I stood my ground.

"Nobody made you take on my route, and after I help you and that's a big IF, you both get to come back home, but I gotta run to church."

Trump card. I had them there. I may have been sleepy, but that Gonder negotiating DNA kicked in faster than adrenaline.

"Oh, you servin' Mass today?" Mark sheepishly replied.

"Yep, at St. Stanislaus, so a large Slurpee AND Doritos or forget it. Going…going…!"

There was a big thumping sound coming from the front porch. We all heard it and knew instantly that it was the bundles of papers being delivered – or rather dumped - near the front door. John broke the silence with a moan.

"There's Spiedel." After that, Mark couldn't back up any further.

"Okay you win, but you 'ain't gettin' nothin' 'til we collect next week. C'mon, John."

As they left the room and went downstairs, I threw aside the blanket I clutched for dear life and jumped into the cold pants, shirt and sweater I'd hung over the headboard of my bunk bed the night before. It should have been snowing as I could faintly see my breath linger in the bedroom air. I yanked on two pairs of socks, tied up my boots and then tiptoed out into the hall just when Dad opened his door, right across from ours, whispering.

"Hey Matt, what are you doing up so early?"

"I'm gonna help Mark and John, and then I gotta serve Mass."

"Better hurry up, then. And you boys keep the noise down. Don't wake the girls."

"Okay."

Downstairs, Mark and John were carrying in and spreading out the heavy newspaper bundles on the floor of the living room. I hated Sunday papers. We all did. They were always three times the usual thickness thanks to the stupid ads. Their weight had already broken or deformed the handlebars on two Stingray bikes so you wonder what they were doing to our backs. But boys are resilient and we somehow survived. I looked out the door. The rain was beating down like a drum onto our wooden front porch.

"Just look at it!" I exclaimed in awe.

"We saw it. That's why we need you, dumb shit."

John always had a special way with words, but before I could voice a defense, Mark jumped in and laid the law.

"C'mon you guys, let's get busy, we ain't got all day."

"Duh."

I admit my reply was lame but I couldn't think of anything better than the multi-purpose phrase all the kids used at school. We sat on the floor and folded the newspapers one by one in our assembly-line formation, snapping a rubber band onto each one and stuffing them into the heavy canvas paperboy ponchos printed with the Oregonian trademark. Our hands were so well trained at this activity we could have done it with our eyes closed. Mark blared out orders to me.

"Matt, you're gonna start over on Greeley Avenue, 'cuz if that guy in the green house doesn't get his paper by six he's gonna yell, then work your way up, do the first block on Killingsworth and I'll meet 'ya on Delaware."

"Okay."

I knew their routes almost as well as they did.

"And be on the lookout in case Spiedel drives by in his white, Chevy coupe. If you see him, just duck behind a car or a tree or anything, but whatever you do, don't let him see you, or he'll start asking you all kinds of stupid questions."

We all chanted loudly in unison: "Spiedel, go to hell."

Dad all but flew down the creaky stairs that squeaked with every step he took.

"Dammit, can't you sons-a-bitches keep your voices down? Gotta wake up the whole Goddamn house?"

Dad always peppered his phrases with lots of harmless colorful expletives to emphasize his points well taken. He never held a grudge, thankfully, so his little quips were over as quickly as they had begun, except when he was under the occasional influence of one drink too many, when his verbal tirades seemed endless.

"Sorry, Dad."

But I wondered how the girls could sleep through his noise, which was much louder than our conversation. He joined us in the living room and looked out the window.

"I'll be damned. It sure is coming down out there."

"And it's freezing, too." John complained in half tones.

"Yeah, Dad, I could see my breath in our bedroom!" Mark whispered loudly.

Dad quietly offered an original comeback.

"Yep, last night it got a little cool."

That sent us into peals of laughter and we repeated the phrase over and over to keep the joke alive.

"It got a little cool!"

"Yep, a little cool."

Dad always had a way of giving any situation a comical or insightful twist, rendering it easier to cope with. We had long ago learned to adapt to living in a house that got "a little cool." Dad kept the thermostat quite low; barely warm enough to appreciate being indoors, and when need be we'd just pop on a sweater or add an extra layer of clothing. Besides, we often had something cooking on the kitchen stove, which offered a snuggly hearth to ward off any chills, and we were all so physically active that we rarely felt the cold.

We continued stretching out the joke and laughing. Dad cut us off.

"Okay now, that's enough. Keep it down."

He climbed over us, singing a familiar chant he loved to vocally exaggerate.

"DON'T get excited."

Dad laughed, entered the kitchen, turned on the oven and put the water pot on the burner before heading out to the bathroom off the back porch to shave. As soon as we had finished the folding phase of our newspaper industry, we made ourselves some toast for breakfast, wrenched into our overstuffed ponchos, adapted to the weight of the paper 'crosses' we had to bear and made way to the door to heed duty's call, out in the colder than "cool" dark dawn wet winter morning.

2. ANYPLACE I HANG MY HAT

Craftsman homes were made with style, boasting ingenious design novelties with nooks and crannies built into every room. Ours had the requisite hardwood floors and a nicely carved staircase that invited you to three bedrooms upstairs, complete with walk-in closets and built-in drawers. Every room was framed in crown moldings and the living room had large windows that opened onto a covered front porch. We had a huge, airy kitchen that seemed more like a second living room, as it was almost the same size as our living room but there were no cupboards on any of the four walls. There was ample space for a long worktable that stood under two tall windows on the east wall in addition to our dining table and six chairs we had centered on the south wall. The door to Aunt Mary's room (the formal dining room that had mahogany built-ins for china and such things we had none of) reigned on the west wall next to the fridge in the corner. On the other side of the fridge was the door to the enclosed back porch, where our broken-down washer and dryer stood in memorial to the lost battle with our dirty clothes, facing the doors to the basement and bathroom. On the east side of the door to the back porch throned the oven, and next to it was a small, walk-in pantry with a double sink below a window that granted full view onto the two enormous Bing cherry trees in the back yard.

The pantry was truly an amazing invention. Once you crossed the threshold, you were welcomed into a tiny room that had cupboards and countertops everywhere, and although ours had definitely seen better days, it had more than its share of character and was perfectly designed for easy access, use and storage with little effort. One windowed cupboard alone offered more than enough space for all the dishes in our possession, and our pots and pans had lots of room to stretch out in the deep cupboards below the counter tops, which also made great hiding places for the occasional game of hide-n-seek. There were three pull-out cutting boards built-in below the counters and even a special deep flour drawer like those used during the early 1900's when the house was built. It was easy to imagine the first lady of the house standing in the middle of the pantry, singing a song as she reaches in and extracts a fist of flour from the pull-drawer to knead her family bread dough on one of the cutting boards. Our family however, was not patterned after tender and traditional Norman Rockwell images. Home-baked bread wasn't on our menu, as sadly, our Mom had passed away from a cerebral hemorrhage in 1962, leaving Dad alone to raise five children between the ages of one to six. It wasn't easy. Dad fought the courts to keep us, as back then in Washington State a widower didn't have custody rights to his own children. In order for us to remain together within the law, we lived for three years with a foster family, followed by two more with Dad's brothers in Spokane and did a short stint in an orphanage before we moved to Chehalis, where Aunt Mary joined our circus. After vagabonding across the state for so long, that old Craftsman in Portland became the first real house we lived in as a family since Mom died, and we were so happy to finally be settled that we didn't miss the home-baked bread. No, like many families in our neighborhood, we bought our white bread pre-baked, sliced and plastic-wrapped, four loaves for eighty-nine cents at the corner market on Killingsworth Street, owned and run by the parents of Heidi Iwata, one of my schoolmates.

Although Dad didn't bake much, he was a great cook and would make us our favorites if he came home early from work, but every weekend without fail he'd be stewing something on the stove for us to enjoy. He'd whip up military-sized quantities of whatever in the huge turkey roaster pan, and it was normal for us to eat chili or chicken and dumplings for two or three days until the roaster was emptied, when we'd resort to the frozen TV dinners and pot-pies we had stocked in the freezer. We didn't mind, as we knew that Dad would soon be cooking up something else, equally as delicious for us to chow down on, which would tide us over for another few days.

We had cupboards in excess for food storage, but I never knew that pantry to be an overflowing cornucopia. There was always something to eat, and naturally you could find plenty of staples on hand for the great comfort foods Dad would cook: packages of spaghetti noodles, canned tomato sauces, large containers of grated parmesan cheese and small tins of Italian seasoning were always on hand for Dad's Bolognese sauce. Large tins of madras curry powder for his chicken curry, Chinese egg noodles and soy sauce for his turkey noodles, bags of long-grain rice, five or six cans each of Campbell's Cream of Mushroom or Cream of Chicken soup that he would use for either pork chops or dumplings. Oatmeal, Cream of Wheat and other boxed cereals were stocked on one shelf, and you found plenty of Kool-Aid near the flavored Jell-O's and puddings we stocked for nighttime TV snacks. Mixed in with the spices on display stood boxes of Kraft macaroni-n-cheese that we would purchase five for a dollar. There were a few cans of green beans, beets, spinach and corn next to a few other stray items that never got eaten but simply resided on the shelves, giving an impression of abundance whenever the staples supply became depleted. Last but not least, the huge metal tin of Empress Strawberry jam and the large jar of Sunny Jim peanut butter eternally held court near the toaster on one of the countertops next to a gooey, sticky knife that had been left out by the 'ghost' we never could name.

Matthew Gonder

3. THE ROAD TO HEAVEN

I didn't cross paths with Spiedel on the route that morning and I was relieved to have delivered to the guy in the green house on Greeley Avenue on time, thus avoiding his wrath. Yet the morning had other surprises in store for me. The rain turned to drizzle as we finished the route. I handed my poncho to Mark and ran like the wind, worried that I'd never make it to church on time. St. Stanislaus, a Catholic Church that served the Polish community in Portland, was almost twenty blocks from our house, way down south on Interstate Avenue. As I raced along, I swear the drivers in their cars made sport of swerving into roadside puddles in order to splash water onto my boots and trousers. Father Joseph met me as I exploded into the Sacristy, completely drenched and out of breath.

"What happened to you, Matthew, my boy? It looks like you went swimming with your clothes on."

I was speechless and panting, afraid he might be upset with me for being late and looking like a wet noodle, but he interrupted my gasps.

"Well, no matter, take off your coat, stand against the heater and dry off as best you can."

"I'm sorry Father. I…did…the…paper route with…my…brothers…"

I choked out the words with what little air I had left in my lungs, compelled to offer an explanation, but he wanted none of it.

"There, there, now relax, it's okay."

"But I gotta… get the Mass…stuff ready!"

"It's all taken care of, Matthew. You just dry off and catch your breath. Tell me, would you like to read the Epistle of St. Luke during Mass?"

"Can I?"

He looked over his glasses into my eyes.

"Luke 1:26. Did you read it at home last night to prepare?"

"Uh, yeah, sure."

I lied. He knew it, but he was also well aware that I was a ham, eager to kill for the chance to speak out into that microphone attached to the podium. Besides, lying to a priest to get onstage could only at worst be a venial, not a mortal sin. No biggie. That meant returning to confession where I'd get a couple of Hail Mary's to recite following an Act of Contrition and my ledger would once again be clean as a whistle, ready to tarnish when the next Epistle needed reading, which would probably be next week.

Father Joseph just smiled at me with compassion, for luckily, everything seemed to amuse him. He handed me the big Bible, with the page marker clearly placed on the page I was to perform - I mean read.

"Here you are then, we haven't much time."

I pressed my dripping backside against the burning hot radiator while I quickly donned my black cassock and white cotta, the standard altar-boy garments. I held my cassock above my waist to allow nothing between my bottom half and the heat, but a few minutes later just as my pants began to sizzle dry, it was time for Mass to begin. I stepped away from the pool of water I had deposited at my feet, grabbed the Bible and followed Father Joseph into the church, making the normal beeline for the altar to genuflect. My boots were still soaked and echoed loud, squishy wet rubber sounds on the marble floor with each step I took, so I overcompensated by tip-toeing in as clouds of steam from my drying trousers floated up and engulfed the air around me. I looked like a 'melting' Wicked Witch of the West and felt conspicuous as if everyone in the church had eyes on me. Father Joe saved me from further embarrassment as he began Mass in his heavy Polish accent, inviting the congregation to give him their undivided attention.

The steam cloud passed soon enough, but stage fright and a pounding heart got the best of me during my Epistle performance – I mean reading. At least I didn't flub any words. I was especially careful to speak extra slowly, enunciating each vowel and syllable to extreme, thoroughly enjoying the sound effects I created with that microphone.

"Thiss issss the wordd of Stt. Lukke."

I loved hearing my voice echo out into the church and wanted to break into song just to see how that would sound, but refrained. Father Joe just rubbed his face to camouflage his chuckles. The rest of the Mass went as usual. I was well rehearsed at the washing of hands, bell-ringing and mixing of water and wine. I had all those gestures down like a dancer knows his choreography. But then came the part of the Mass I always dreaded. Communion. No, I never understood nor could stomach that part. From where I stood, it totally grossed me out big time. Every time. And here it came again: a hundred people or more, all lined up, approaching Father Joseph and me as we stood in front of the altar. One behind the other they came at us like zombies, and I had to hold a silver plate under each chin while Father Joe offered a Communion host, then watch them close their eyes and stick out their veiny, lumpy, stringy or foamy, saliva-covered tongues, breathing God knows how many infectious germs in our faces. I wanted to wretch on many occasions, especially when I witnessed a "writher"; what I called a tongue that never stopped moving once the proprietor protruded it out. And if it accidentally touched Father Joseph's finger, I would cringe and gag. Knowing he had to continue handing out Communion to others after someone's yucky tongue scraped his finger nauseated me, since I knew he was passing those same filthy germs on to everyone else in the church. I had nightmares after discovering some of the most hideous dental work and decay I care to remember in those overstretched, open buccal cavities. Who came up with a Communion ceremony like that anyway?

We would get punished for sticking our tongues out at anyone, so why was it okay to do it to nice old Father Joe? He wasn't a masochist. No wonder the Catholics had written Mass in such a way that the priest got to take a big swig of wine before Communion. Believe me, he needed it bad.

After Communion, Father Joseph blessed everyone and the church emptied out, except for the ardent few who remained behind in silent prayer. Once we had returned to the Sacristy, I put everything away as fast as I could, grabbed my coat that had dried during Mass, said goodbye to Father Joe and ran home.

4. 'TIS THE SEASON

When I arrived, John was napping on the couch. I walked into the kitchen where Monica and Marguerite sat at the table drinking hot chocolate and eating cinnamon toast. It was Mark's turn to do the dishes, and to my amazement - instead of paying someone else to do them - he was actually carrying greasy pots from the stove to the sink in the pantry to wash up. Dad was nowhere to be seen, so I inquired:

"Hi guys, how come you didn't come to Mass?"

Mark cocked his head toward Aunt Mary's room.

"Dad's been in there all morning."

I suddenly heard the classical music that filled the house, a clear sign that Aunt Mary was coming out of her downer and would soon be back to her bubbly self.

"Oh."

Marguerite held up her cup of hot chocolate.

"Hey Matt, you want some Swiss piss?"

What do you expect from kids? That's what Dad called our favorite hot chocolate powder one day, and the name stuck.

"I'll make some for ya, if ya want," Monica offered graciously.

Before I could answer her, the door opened to Aunt Mary's room and Dad emerged. All eyes went to him for the verdict. He nodded his head and we knew the storm had passed.

"Who wants spaghetti?" he announced.

"I do" everyone yelped in unison.

"How're them dishes comin' along, Mark?" Dad inquired.

"I'm almost done," came Mark's defensive reply.

We all watched and assisted Dad as he pulled hamburger meat from the fridge and started frying it up in an extra large cast-iron skillet, tossing in spices, tomato sauce and onions without measuring a thing. The thyme and oregano in the Italian seasoning embalmed the kitchen, and we all knew we'd be taking turns, secretly swiping spoonfuls of sauce throughout the day as it stewed on the stove. Then Dad started teasing us.

"Aunt Mary wants me to drive downtown and pick up this years' Firestone Christmas album for her collection. Who wants to go with me?"

Marguerite was the first to bite the bait.

"I do, but can we get our Christmas tree, too, Dad, please Dad, please?"

Dad poured oil onto her fire.

"Christmas tree? We don't need a Christmas tree. We had one last year that just dried up and died, and besides, there's too much furniture in the living room. We don't have room for a Christmas tree."

That got Marguerite going even more.

"Yeah we do. Next to the TV by the window."

Marguerite ran into the living room and pointed right where the tree should stand.

"See, right here!"

Dad continued toying as she danced about.

"Weellll…. let's see, we might be able to squeeze a small one in there."

"A small one?" she protested. "No, a great big one, way up to the ceiling!"

"A big one? I don't know 'bout that."

"C'mon, Dad."

He'd had his share of fun and deemed it time to get down to details.

"Who knows where the lights and decorations are?"

I was the organizer of the family and knew where everything was, excluding objects lost in our bedroom junk.

"I do. They're under the stairs in the basement."

"Well, go grab 'em and let's take a look at what we got that still works."

Marguerite felt as if she'd won a victory and jumped around.

"Hooray, we're gonna get our Christmas tree, Monica, we're gettin' our Christmas tree!"

Monica, Marguerite and I went out onto the back porch and opened the door to the basement. We stepped down the old wooden staircase and reached under the stairs, pulling out the boxes of decorations that still had remnants of snow flocking from last year's abuse. We carried our treasures upstairs and arrayed the contents on the kitchen floor. Dad pulled out the string of lights and plugged it into a nearby socket, testing each bulb with Mark.

"Looks like some of these bulbs are shot, Mark. Count up how many we need." He said.

My sisters and I were more intrigued by the old glass colored balls and family heirloom decorations in the boxes, each one stirring up memories in our hearts of Christmas' past.

"Remember this one Aunt Fran gave us?" Monica exclaimed.

"Oh, this one's my favorite," Marguerite wailed, pulling out an angel covered in glitter.

Unfortunately, there was always at least one decoration that didn't survive.

"Oh shoot, this one's broke," I announced sadly.

"Yeah well, shit happens on the move out West," came Dad's reliable reply, making us all laugh.

He used that phrase often to teach us to roll with the punches life threw our way. Dad gave the spaghetti sauce a last stir, turning the burner down to a low simmer. Mark had finished his broken bulb count.

"Fourteen, Dad."

"Fourteen? Okay, let's get a move on. Everyone hop in the car!"

"But John's sleeping on the couch." Monica said.

"Well, go wake him up, Monica, and ask him if he wants to go. If he doesn't, we'll just let him sleep."

Monica ran into the living room and gave John a nudge.

"John, you wanna go with us to get our Christmas tree?"

John stirred, hearing every word.

"Mmm? Yeah, I guess so."

"Well c'mon then, better get up, we're leaving now." Monica added.

We grabbed our coats, ran out the door and piled into Dad's Mercury Comet.

Downtown, we ran all the errands we had on our list, collecting the bulbs, icicles and various items we needed. We peered into some of the holiday windows the department stores had dressed to generate a festive atmosphere and entice kids to want the new toys on display, but we didn't fall for that commercial ploy. We mentioned the different things we thought we might want for Christmas, knowing Dad, our Santa, would get us each one gift, and one gift only. Then we drove to five different gas stations to find that damn Firestone collector record, but the stocks were always depleted. You had to be an early bird if you wanted one of those worms. The acquisition of that record became a mission Dad refused to fail in order to raise his sister's spirit, so we fought the traffic further on until we finally found a gas station that had a few copies left. Relieved to put that behind us, we had one last stop to make, which purchase our Christmas tree. Dad pulled into the parking lot of a store that boasted a makeshift tree farm with twinkling lights trailing from post to post and a big painted sign promoting trees of all shapes, sizes and varieties. He knew exactly the kind of tree he was looking for, as usual, a Douglas fir with space between the branches in order to give room for the silver-lead icicles he loved so much. He finally chose the one he wanted, with our help, of course. He paid the salesman, and once we had secured and tied it to the roof of the car, we all jumped in. We drove home in a state of holiday bliss, singing carols 'all the way' while keeping an eye out to make sure our tree didn't slide off the roof.

Once Dad had parked the car in front of our house, Mark and John untied the tree while Marguerite, Monica and I carried in the sacks of other stuff. Dad proudly clutched the prized Firestone Christmas record under his arm, and as we walked through the front door, Aunt Mary sat rocking away in her chair, looking drawn and remorseful. Dad handed her the record and smiled as her face lit up.

"Oh WONDERFUL, you found it," she squealed in her high-pitched voice.

"Put it on, Mary. Let's hear it while the kids decorate the tree."

"Right away, Seamus, gee thanks," she said, calling Dad by the nickname she gave him.

Dad silently smiled at her. She jumped out of her rocker as she ripped off the cellophane wrapping and placed it with care onto the stereo record player against the wall. Mark and John were yanking and pulling the tree through the front door.

"Over here, boys," Dad directed, pulling the chair away from the window.

"Matt, get down there and center that tree stand on the floor, right there."

I fell to my knees, placed the stand where he directed and then got out of the way. Then Dad took on the big maneuver; he lifted the tree up while Mark, on all fours, guided the trunk into the stand. Mark and John then twisted the screws on the four sides of the stand, securing it in good and tight. Dad added a crank or two to the screws just to be sure and then we all stood back in awe, admiring the new addition that permeated the familiar scent of fresh pine to our home.

Suddenly the needle hit the vinyl and Christmas music flooded the house. The holiday season had officially begun. Dad attached the lights to the branches as we sang the old Christmas songs we cherished along with Bing Crosby, Danny Kaye, Doris Day, Mahalia Jackson, the Brothers Four, Julie

Andrews and many others. We hung all the brightly colored glass balls and decorations, and then Dad made us hang the silver tinsel on the tree one strand at a time, branch by branch. We toiled laboriously, taking breaks from time to time to discreetly steal spoons of spaghetti sauce from the skillet on the stove. That icicle job seemed to linger on forever, but to Dad, that was the only way to do it right.

Aunt Mary watched us work, drinking coffee and smoking as she rocked away in musical bliss to the operatic tenor Robert Merrill singing Ave Maria. Aunt Mary was from the old school of music. At one time, she seemed destined to become a concert pianist and had trained years to reach her dream. However, life dealt her another hand of cards and she became one of the most sought-after surgical nurses in the Pacific Northwest, gifted with an intuitive foresight as to what instruments the surgeon needed before being asked. Jobs were offered to her wherever she chose to live, but she had a soft heart and would fall into depression when she witnessed people she cared for suffering, hence the periodic binges with John Barleycorn. She never married for lack of falling in love, so, being Dad's favorite sister, she lived with us for a few years. She had her share of demons to say the least, but it was nice to have a woman's presence around again, and comforting to not come home every day from school to an empty house. She was a character and we all loved her. Not only was she good to us kids but she opened up the world of music for me. She had literally thousands of records in the collection lined up against the walls in her room, and exposed me to everything from Mozart, Beethoven, Bach and Rachmaninov to singing groups of yodelers from the Swiss Alps.

But right then, as we continued stringing the icicles, I watched the blood drain from her classically trained hands as she suddenly clenched the armrests on her rocking chair, when Barbra Streisand began singing The Lord's Prayer. By the tight look on her face, I thought Aunt Mary was going to have a seizure, but after Streisand held that last emotional note in her powerful rendition, Aunt Mary, mesmerized in her rocking rhythm, screamed: "PLAY IT AGAIN!"

I ran to the stereo and picked up the needle, placing it at the beginning of the track. Aunt Mary listened as if in a trance, and I had to "Play it again" five times before she was ready to let us move on to another song by someone else. The blend of The Lord's Prayer and Streisands' voice seemed to magically purge her pain. Satisfied, Aunt Mary gulped down her black coffee, jumped up and flew to the kitchen, where she began whipping up chocolate-chip walnut cookie dough. She tripled the batch and stood there at the worktable stirring away while we completed our tinsel task. A half-hour and several hundred silver strands later we had finished to Dad's approval, and then he sprayed a few cans of flocked snow onto the branches, topping each one in a thick blanket of white. We all stood back in admiration. The flocking covered some of the light bulbs, giving the impression that it had really snowed in our living room, and the effect was a sight to behold.

By this time, Aunt Mary was pulling cookie sheets out of the oven, happy as a lark, lining up the hot cookies on tea towels. Dad let us have a few while they were warm, but he knew his little vultures would descend and devour every cookie if he didn't take charge, so he put the noodles on to boil and served up the spaghetti feast.

After dinner, we all sat around the tree in the living room and watched 'A Charlie Brown Christmas' on our black and white TV, all the while stuffing stacks of fresh cookies and milk into our mouths as Aunt Mary and Dad rocked away in their chairs. After Charlie Brown was over, we surfed among the three stations we had and watched whatever was on until the Sandman claimed us. Those who were still able tottered off to bed. The others, me included, were carried up the stairs in Dad's arms.

5. YOU'VE GOT TO BE TAUGHT

The next morning was Monday, and fortunately for me it didn't rain, so Mark and John did the paper route alone. Afterwards, all dressed in our uniforms, we walked the ten blocks to our old, red brick Catholic school. As John and I entered our classroom at Blessed Sacrament Elementary (the fifth and sixth grades shared a large room together), Sister Raphael was busy speedwriting on the chalkboard and rolling down maps of the world in preparation for our day. She scribbled vigorously without turning around as she sang out "Good Morning," to which the whole class responded an automatic "Good Morning Sister Raphael" in unison. She wore down chalk at such a rapid pace that we knew we'd better buckle down and concentrate or get lost in the shuffle. She was a steadfast educator with a formal demeanor in her black and white habit that demanded respect, yet she sincerely loved children and it showed. We settled at our desks, saluting our friends silently until she faced us, smiling warmly from the heart. She folded her hands in prayer and we immediately jumped up and stood erect as trained soldiers to recite our daily prayer followed by the salute to the flag. Then we sat down and Sister Raphael made an announcement.

"As we approach the Christmas season, it is time for us as good Catholics and citizens to show extra kindness to others. We are all very lucky here, but there are many around us who do not have enough to eat. For this reason we are hosting a food drive."

During her speech, she walked over to one of the bulletin boards and yanked on a map that rolled up like a blind, revealing a colorful sign she had pinned up that read:

BLESSED SACRAMENT

CHRISTMAS FOOD DRIVE

Week 1: pasta, rice, dried beans, lentils, noodles

Week 2: flour, sugar, powdered milk, cereals,crackers

Week 3: canned fruits and vegetables, tomato sauces

+ 10 cents per student to buy turkeys and perishables…fresh milk, butter, eggs, cheese, etc.

Armed with her long wooden pointing stick with the black rubber tip like a magic wand, she tapped the list.

"We're asking that every week starting with this one, each student bring in and donate one item from the list and place it in the box right here."

She aimed her pointer beneath the sign on the floor, where sat a large empty cardboard box wrapped like a Christmas gift. As Sister Raphael continued, she pointed to the Sacred Heart of Jesus piggy bank sitting on her desk.

"And finally, we're asking for a donation of ten cents per student to buy fresh turkeys and perishable items like butter, milk, cheese et cetera. Once we've collected everything, our Parish volunteers will deliver the boxes before Christmas to the poor, so they will be able to enjoy their holiday just like you and me."

My heart sank. I thought of the two piled-up plates of spaghetti and all the cookies I had eaten the night before and felt sad that others didn't have the same as we did at our house. My mind flashed on Renata and her two sisters who lived with their single Mom across the street from us. They always had holes in their worn-out clothes, very little furniture and barely enough to eat. If anyone deserved to receive free food, they were definitely candidates for kindness. Sister Raphael emphasized her point.

"So, as you can see, this week, each of you bring in one package of pasta or rice or dried beans, lentils, noodles or another dry food item and place it in the box. I'm handing each of you a mimeographed note for you to give to your parents that will explain everything clearly."

She grabbed a pile of papers from her desk and handed them to one student, who took one sheet and passed on the rest. Without missing a beat, Sister Raphael segued to our first lesson.

"God Bless you. Please take out your maps of Africa."

I loved Geography. Sister Raphael taught us so much about every country; what each one produced, the population, the government structure, what people wore, customs and religions. We drew out the shapes of each country in colored pencils to help us situate its placement on the globe clearly in our minds. To this day I think of her and although I haven't traveled the entire planet yet, I can, in my mind's eye, still see many countries on the hand-made maps I drew for her.

That lesson took us to our Math lesson, where we were learning how to multiply ratios. Then Sister Amelia, our singing nun, joined us to rehearse the songs scheduled for midnight Mass on Christmas Eve. We ate lunch and played out in the schoolyard, and then the afternoon took off where one lesson led to the next. Before we realized it, the day had passed and we were walking home.

Aunt Mary was in her chair rocking away when we clamored through the front door. She greeted us warmly, asking how our day went, and it was so nice to see her feeling better, gazing at our tree while she listened to an unending mix of Christmas music. We had leftover spaghetti sauce to heat up for dinner and there were lots of cookies laying in rows on the worktable yet to scoff up. It was John's turn to do the dishes, but he wasn't in the mood, so he asked Marguerite.

"Hey Marguerite, ya wanna do my dishes for ten cents?"

Her bartering skills were better than anyone else's. Without even looking in the pantry, she began her third grade master-level negotiating process.

"Ten? What are you, crazy? You see how many dishes there are? Gimme twenty."

"Fifteen?"

Marguerite was ready to chew on that piece of gristle all night if need be to win.

"Look at all those pots and pans. That spaghetti sauce is stuck everywhere. Twenty."

John was too tired to fight and knew it was hopeless anyway.

"Okay."

"Pay me now."

He coughed up the cash and Marguerite got to work, scrubbing away. About the time we were finishing up our dinner and Marguerite the clean-up, we heard Dad coming through the front door.

"Hi Dad," we all chorused from the kitchen, welcoming him home.

"Howdy," he answered, joining us, carrying a large plastic laundry basket and two sacks of groceries in his arms. We knew what that meant and enthusiastically responded in kind.

"The Christmas basket…hooray…yeah, Dad!"

He handed the groceries to Aunt Mary, who took them into the pantry to put away. Dad carried his basket and we followed him into the living room. He placed the basket down next to the tree and we all knew what was coming next. We waited for his orders. Aunt Mary arrived and sat in her rocker to enjoy the show. Dad began.

"Monica, Marguerite, you girls cover the inside of the basket with wrapping paper. Boys, there are more sacks in the back seat of the car."

My sisters pulled out the rolls of decorated wrapping paper from under the tree, while us boys ran outside to the curb where Dad had parked the Comet. Just as the girls had finished layering the paper inside the basket, we returned laden with grocery bags that we placed on the floor. All five of us sat around the basket and Dad began preparing our favorite annual Christmas tradition. Ten little hands extended over the top of the basket to mix up the goodies as he poured in one after the other: Brazil nuts, caramels, walnuts, licorice, almonds, gummy candies, pecans, tangerines, hazel nuts, mixed hard candy, oranges, bananas, toffees, candy canes, apples and chocolates. We mixed everything up as quickly as he added each new ingredient, filling the basket to the brim. Dad went into the kitchen and grabbed two nutcrackers and shoved them into the basket. He then placed seven boxes of chocolate covered cherries beneath the tree, one whole box for each member of the family. We truly cherished our annual basket that sat under the tree offering goodies all throughout the winter for us to nibble on whenever we wanted a snack. We'd attack that basket like termites when we returned home from school or were lying on the floor watching the annual Christmas TV shows. Day after day we ate our way through most of the contents, leaving only a few Brazil nuts at the bottom, as they were the hardest to crack open. By the end of the holiday season, the wrapping paper would eventually become torn and worn for wear, the basket would replace the worn-out one in our laundry room, and there was nothing left but those chocolate covered cherries to nibble on. Unfortunately, our memory bones were connected to our stomach bones and we held off consuming those chocolate cherries for as long as we could, because one year all five of us kids had gotten sick from eating too many too quickly. The thought of eating even one chocolate covered cherry turned our stomachs. We didn't have the heart to ask Dad not to buy them anymore because they reminded him of his childhood memories that he was so happy to share with us. So, reluctantly, we caved in but would eat them slowly. Very slowly. We usually had a box or two that lasted until April.

6. SCHOOL DAZE

The next morning, Dad had left early for work and Aunt Mary was still asleep. Mark and John were on the paper route and my sisters and I were uniformed, sitting at the table eating oatmeal and talking as quietly as possible, without much success. Caught up in all the excitement of our Christmas basket, we realized we'd forgotten to mention the Food Drive to Dad. No problem. I was used to forging Dad's signature when needed on school papers, so I was confident that I could handle this one easy enough without bothering him. We carried our cereal bowls into the pantry, placed them in the sink and looked into the cupboards to check the inventory.

"Good thing Dad went shopping last night" I said, discovering the food Aunt Mary had put away.

I gave Marguerite a pack of Rice-a-Roni, then grabbed two bags of dried red beans from one shelf, handed one to Monica and placed two bags of long grain rice on the counter for Mark and John to take. We gathered our coats, leaving Aunt Mary to enjoy a house full of peace and quiet and walked our ten blocks to school.

Once I arrived in my classroom, I deposited my bag of beans in the big box under the Food Drive sign while Sister Raphael burned chalk on the board. I was happy to see that many other students had remembered to bring an offering as well. Right as we began the daily prayer, John burst through the door to our classroom. Sister Raphael knew about the paper route, so she just gave him a nod as he tossed his bag of rice into the box and took position next to his desk, joining the rest of us. Once she began her morning announcements, Sister Raphael blessed and thanked the classroom for our generosity and positive response to the Food Bank project and then got on with the English lessons she had chalked onto the board like Speedy Gonzales.

Later at home that afternoon, the spaghetti sauce had become a distant memory, so we knew we'd have to fend for ourselves and eat frozen TV dinner's that night. I preferred the fried chicken dinners as the Salisbury steak gave me the impression that I was eating someone's sliced dog in brown gravy. After dinner, it was my turn to do the dishes but I got lucky, as there weren't many, thanks to the disposable, aluminum TV dinner trays. As soon as I washed up the few dishes I had, I joined the others lounging around watching TV, while Aunt Mary rocked away, putting her hair up in pin-curls, informing us in her inimitable voice that she was returning to work the next day. I knew that meant we'd see her in her white uniform and nurse's hat running to catch the bus.

The rest of the week went by uneventfully. Dad and Aunt Mary went to work as usual. Mark, John and I did the rounds on the route and collected the $2.80 fee from our clients that received the paper everyday. Mark paid up my salary of $2.25 (a quarter for every day I did the route in November) and he bought me the Slurpee and Doritos he promised me for helping out that rainy Sunday. There were some funny folks we encountered when we collected, as they were all generally asleep when we delivered the paper every morning. That man in the green house on Greeley always coughed up his payment with a verbal warning to make sure we kept on delivering his paper before six a.m. John was, as usual, pilfering cookies from old ladies while he collected on his route, while another client, Old Mr. Johnson, always turned the moment into a comic routine for Mark and me.

We rang his doorbell and waited. He answered, peeking out from behind the screen door in a fake state of shock.

"Yes, what is it?"

Mark gave him the canned response. I stood back silently enjoying the scene.

"Hi Mr. Johnson. We're collecting for the Oregonian."

Mr. Johnson pretended not to hear or understand even though he recognized the same boys he saw every month, so he came out onto the porch to play it up.

"What did you say?"

Mark knew his lines and spoke louder.

"Mr. Johnson, we're collecting for the Oregonian! You know, the newspaper. For November."

Johnson cupped his hand to his ear.

"The Oregonian, you say? What a terrible waste of time, paper and money. That newspaper is full of bad news, and especially last November. I shouldn't have to pay for it."

We laughed. Johnson was happy. He had an audience and continued his stand-up act.

"Well, how much you want?"

"Two dollars and eighty cents," Mark answered.

"What? Two-eighty?"

"Yeah, same as last month."

"Two-eighty, that's highway robbery."

We laughed on cue as he reached into his pocket and pulled out a ten-dollar bill.

"You got change for a ten?"

"Sure do," Mark said, reaching into his pocket and pulling out a wad of cash and checks that other clients had given him. One five-dollar bill fell from the wad onto the porch. Johnson was ready for it.

"Ah, don't worry about that. Just leave it. I gotta sweep the porch anyway."

We cracked up as Mark reached down to grab the five. Johnson stretched it.

"I said don't over exert yourself. I'll clean it up later."

"Yeah, sure you will."

Mark handed Johnson the correct change. Johnson smiled as Mark and I laughed.

"Thanks, Mr. Johnson. See ya next month."

"Okay, boys, you take care now."

And with his last phrase, he waved us goodbye and went back inside.

Finally Saturday arrived, bringing the first herald of the season. Although we had grown immune to the Portland rain, we were all thrilled to witness what should have been raindrops fall slowly from the sky in fluffy white flakes. I got bullied into helping Mark and John on the paper route, which I didn't mind for once because it was an adventure to finally stroll those familiar streets under snowfall. Kids from all over the neighborhood were outside early that day enjoying themselves, and although most of it melted as soon as it hit the ground, enough had settled on the parked cars to scrape up a snowball or two to toss, and with it came the hope of more to come. After all, Bing Crosby didn't own the patent on dreaming of a White Christmas.

Back home after the papers were delivered, Dad and Aunt Mary were rocking away, talking about this 'n that as they gulped down cups of coffee and smoked cigarettes. Monica and Marguerite were watching cartoons on TV and munching on the basket goodies. As soon as we returned from the route and tossed our ponchos into a corner, Dad barked out an announcement.

"Hey, who's in the mood for chili this weekend?"

He didn't have to wait long for a response, especially from John who was reputed to having an empty leg and a bottomless pit for a stomach.

"I am," came his retort, mixed with everyone else's affirmation.

"Okey dokey, then I'll get it started and we'll have it tomorrow," he smiled.

Dad gave himself a heavy rock in his chair that deposited him onto his feet. He passed through the kitchen into the pantry and opened the cupboard to discover there were no red beans on the shelf. He called out.

"What the hell? Mary, didn't I buy beans last Sunday?"

Aunt Mary stopped rocking long enough to ponder.

"You did, Seamus. I remember putting two bags on the shelf."

Dad opened up all the cupboards, not finding what he was looking for, and frustrated, slammed the doors shut. Monica and I, suddenly remembering what we had done, glanced at each other and ran into the kitchen to explain.

"Dad, I forgot to tell you. We gave them to the Food Drive at school," I admitted.

"Food Drive, what the hell is that?" Dad inquired with frustration as he opened another cupboard.

"We all have to bring food each week to school to help feed the poor," I said.

"So they can have Christmas, too," Monica added in my defense.

"What the hell are you two jabbering on about?" Dad demanded, unsatisfied.

"Wait a second, Dad, I got a letter for you from Sister Raphael that explains it."

I ran upstairs and grabbed the letter from the book bag in my bedroom, flew back down the stairs and ran through the living room into the kitchen, handing it to Dad.

"What is this happy horseshit?"

He snatched it from me and read on, his frustration diminishing when he finally understood. But then I could see him doing the math in his head.

"Okay, but this means five items per week? That's fifteen food items plus fifty cents? Well shit, if we give everything we have to the poor, what the hell are we supposed to eat?"

Then he got a bright idea.

"Tell you what, you kids have two weeks left on this shenanigan, right? Next week why don't three of you take something in to the Food Bank, and the following week the other two can bring something else, okay? That way you each skip one week. I don't mind helping out but we can't afford to feed the whole Goddamn world, or we'll all be goin' over to their Goddamn house for dinner. Fair Enough?"

"Okay, Dad, sounds good." What else could I say?

"And next time, try to take 'em something we don't need. I'll be damned. And you can each give a damn - dime - from your own pocket. That way we ALL participate. So now what the hell are we supposed to do today about our chili?"

I offered my services.

"I'll run up to Iwata's and get more beans, Dad. I'll go right now."

He pulled a five-dollar bill from his wallet and handed it to me.

"Jesus Christ. This here money doesn't grow on trees, ya know. Okay, get three bags of red beans, and while you're at it, better pick up four more loaves of bread."

Just when his flame began to extinguish, Marguerite stirred the coals.

"We're outa jam, too, Dad," she informed.

Dad peered into the Empress Strawberry jam tin sitting on the counter.

"What the hell you mean we're outa jam? There's a whole quarter tin left."

"That's not jam, Dad, that's just the bees," she answered, meekly.

Here it came. Marguerite did it good. Dad exploded.

"Bees? BEES? What the hell do you mean, bees?"

Poor Marguerite did the best she could to offer her explanation.

"I don't like those lumps at the bottom. It's like eating bees."

That did it. Dad totally lost it.

"BEES? Those lumps are whole Goddamn strawberries for Chris'sake! That there's good quality jam! Bees!"

Marguerite started to cry.

"Nevermind, I'll eat 'em, Dad, I'm sorry," she blubbered.

I decided to run out the door and get the beans before Dad popped a valve. I ran to Iwata's, two blocks away up on Killingsworth Street, bought the beans and bread, and bee-lined my way home, excuse the pun. Dad was in the kitchen waiting for me.

Marguerite and Monica had forgotten the bee episode and were laughing as they played cards at the table. I handed Dad the beans that he poured into the roaster pan, covering them in cold water.

"These beans have got to soak overnight. So it's pot-pies for you kids tonight, and we'll have the chili tomorrow."

Nobody dared complain.

"That's okay, Dad," Mark said.

"I wonder what the poor are eating this weekend," Dad added thoughtfully.

We didn't know whether we should laugh or be silent until we heard him laughing to himself, answering his own question.

"Probably beans and bees. I'll be damned. Bees."

The thought now tickled him. We ate the pot-pies, watched more TV that night and again made another dent in the Christmas basket while Dad and Aunt Mary rocked and smoked until we hobbled off to bed.

Sunday came and with it more rain and heavy papers to deliver. Yes, I got goaded into helping my brothers, but by the time we had finished folding the papers and fastening the rubber bands, Dad was in the kitchen browning hamburger meat, adding chili pepper and other spices to the red beans that had soaked overnight. We could hardly wait to finish the paper route and come home to that roaster pan full of chili.

The route took us so long, but fortunately none of us were scheduled to serve Mass that day. When we burst through the front door, Aunt Mary, drinking her coffee and rocking away to Christmas music, greeted us.

"Good Morning, Matt, Mark and John."

"Hi Aunt Mary," we all responded in kind.

"Sorry we're too late for Mass," I said to her.

"Never you mind," she answered. Then she announced the news.

"Guess who's coming next Thursday to visit us, Matt?"

Could have been anyone, but I guessed right.

"Father Blaes?"

"How did you know?" Aunt Mary inquired.

"I didn't, but that's great," was my response.

Although the news of his visit pleased everyone, at that particular moment, Dad's chili smelled so incredible, beckoning us to the kitchen. We ran to the pantry, grabbed bowls and ladled up from the turkey roaster on the stove again and again throughout the afternoon and sat at the table, gobbling away. Dad always got a kick watching us scarf up his food.

That night while we watched TV, Aunt Mary told Dad she would be taking a few days off from work during Father Blaes' visit. Dad, not being the handy-man type, asked if she would be willing to deal with a repairman to get our broken clothes washer back to functioning order. She said she would handle it and make the call the next morning, happy to rid us of the drudge of weekly Laundromat duties.

7. WINTER BLAZES

The new week began like the last, and with it came more of the same activities under more rainy skies that drizzled endless tears of rebellion on our hopes of a white Christmas. Adhering to Dad's directive, Mark, John and Marguerite each brought a food item to school that week for the Food Drive. Monica and I, empty handed, discreetly gave the big boxes in our classrooms a stir to give the impression that we were doing our Christian duty. No one noticed we didn't actually put something in, and although I felt guilty about it, I obeyed Dad's orders. Then I got an idea as to how I could save face. I saw the Jesus piggy bank sitting on Sister Raphael's desk, so I dug a dime out of my pocket, walked over and pushed it through the slot in Jesus' back, satisfied at last to not appear as if I wasn't doing my good Catholic citizen share.

On Thursday, as Aunt Mary, in her uniform muumuu and slippers, was home readying the house for Father Blaes' visit, the repairman had arrived and was out on the back porch stretched out on the floor behind the washing machine he had pushed up against the door to the basement. After he'd been there a couple of hours, Aunt Mary began to get edgy. She opened the door to the back porch and called out to the man. Her high-pitched voice took on an Irish accent whenever she got herself fired up.

"Excuse me, sir, but you've been down there a very long time. Are you going to be much longer?"

"These things take time, ma'am," the repairman grumbled.

"I understand, but you're blocking my way to the basement and I have to get down there and make a bed for my houseguest who's arriving very soon today."

"I'm just trying to do my job," came his ludicrous response.

"SO AM I," growled Aunt Mary.

The repairman tried to defend himself.

"I'm trying to find the problem and be thorough, here, ma'am."

"Well be quick about it, then, will you?" she said, slamming the door shut.

Twenty minutes or so later, the repairman entered the kitchen, looking drawn. Aunt Mary was fit to be tied.

"Well?" She charged in an accusing tone.

"I found this in the dryer."

The repairman handed her a cast iron skillet encrusted with dried-on, molded spaghetti sauce that Marguerite hid in the dryer a week ago to avoid scrubbing. Aunt Mary, having witnessed Marguerite's routine many times before, snatched it and shook it at him, repeating herself.

"Well?"

The repairman was timid and non-committal.

"Well, there's a number of things that need replacing, but that's to be expected from a machine this old."

Aunt Mary had lost all patience and yelled at him.

"Well, can you or can you NOT fix it, man?"

The poor bastard tried to respond calmly, but probably began fearing for his life.

"I'll have to order some parts. We don't stock everyth..."

She cut him off.

"And how long will that take?"

He was becoming visibly shaken, as she could be forceful when need be.

"A few days. If I put the order in today, I should have them by Monday."

She continued to charge at him.

"Well, then be at it, Man, will you? Now that you've spent two hours and twenty minutes finding the problems, it shouldn't take you that long to replace the new parts, should it? Jesus, Mary and Joseph, I can perform exploratory surgery on the human body faster than you can diagnose a broken washing machine!"

He started shaking in his boots.

"It should only take me about half an hour to replace the new parts."

She guided him to the front door.

"Fine. Then I'll be expecting you on Monday. You're charging me sixteen dollars an hour and we're not Rockefellers and I'll be DAMNED if I'm taken for a fool!"

He scurried out the front door like a puppy with his tail between his legs. Aunt Mary collected herself and made up Father Blaes' bed in the basement in plenty of time before he arrived.

Father Blaes (pronounced Blaze) was an amazing man. A Jesuit priest who taught Latin and Religion at Bellarmine High School in Tacoma, he was one of the kindest men I have ever met, and we considered him a member of our family. He had been friends with Aunt Mary and Dad since their days at Gonzaga University, and would appear out of God knows where and join us for a few days wherever we were living every once in a while. We had no guest room so he slept in the dirt floor basement on a makeshift bed but never complained, and would take long solitary walks everyday to meditate and pray. Not only was he a priest, but he was also a skilled carpenter. He would always arrive carrying tools and repair whatever needed his attention during his stay with us to make our lives more comfortable. When Dad bought us Stingray bikes for Christmas one year, Father Blaes built us a bike rack to park them. Another time, when we lived in Chehalis in our singlewide trailer with the 'expando' living room, Father Blaes built a skirt around the foundation to protect the pipes and wheels. He was always fixing something. And he taught John and me how to serve Mass. I'll never forget that day. He had a "sink or swim" training method, which basically consisted of saying a normal Mass, in Latin for God's sake, and snapping his fingers and pointing at whatever he wanted us to do. We were given no preparation beforehand. We donned our cassocks and jumped in the holy water, so to speak. When the time came, Father Blaes simply snapped his fingers and pointed at the water and wine when we were supposed to pour. He snapped his fingers and pointed at the bells when it was time to ring them. He snapped and pointed where he wanted us to stand or when we were to approach him, and we looked like untrained seals in front of a church full of people staring at us. Once you made it through that humiliation, you learned how to serve Mass and could almost speak Latin. Under his direction, it only took one Mass looking like a retarded altar boy to learn how to guess his needs prior to his snapping and pointing. Maybe that's why I can't stand anyone pointing at me to this day.

Father Blaes loved pork roast and we had one in his honor every time he came to visit. He shared a common sense of humor with Dad and Aunt Mary and they would laugh for hours on end at everything. One hot summer day in Chehalis, Father Blaes declined the invitation to stay for dinner, got up from his chair and announced he was returning to his monastery to cool off. When Dad asked why he was leaving so early, he answered:

"I can't stand the heat. Us Blaes'es get pretty hot."

We arrived home from school that Thursday afternoon to find Dad, Aunt Mary and Father Blaes like always cackling at life's absurdities in the living room. Padre, as Dad called him, asked us kids details of our current scholastic and ecclesiastic events, but there was something odd about his inquisitive manner this particular time. Normally, he never asked for details but was satisfied to get a simple, general lowdown on what we were doing. I had the feeling that something was up but let it go. Later that evening, we all sat around the table in the kitchen as

Father Blaes said grace, blessed the family and the pork roast. We all started to chow down while Aunt Mary's Christmas music played endlessly to everyone's delight throughout the meal. But when I heard Nat King Cole sing "The Little Boy that Santa Claus Forgot," I completely lost my appetite. I felt so guilty to be sitting at that table full of food as Nat King Cole sang of a little boy who didn't have a daddy and had nothing but broken toys to play with, and I didn't even bring in something for the food drive that week. I just sat there and toyed with my meal because I couldn't swallow a thing.

After dinner we all sat in the living room and Dad barked at me for having my feet on the couch. Once we hit a commercial break, Dad announced that Father Blaes had something for us kids. We figured it was a probably a new container for holy water or a rosary, but were surprised to say the least, when we discovered what he brought. He opened a brown paper bag and pulled out a strange contraption that resembled a metal octopus with a tubular copper head attached to a dozen two-feet rubber-coated wires flogging about like tentacles. He handed it to Dad, who took the floor.

"I asked Padre to make something to help me solve some problems your Aunt Mary and I have been having lately."

We looked at Father Blaes in wonder, as we'd never expected something like that to come out of a priest's brown paper gift bag. Dad continued.

"I've asked you kids time and time again to keep your damn feet off the couch that's wearing out from your shoes. I come home many nights and the dishes aren't washed. There hasn't been a day that two or more of you are fighting in the house, screaming at the top of your lungs, and it's high time we put an end to all this happy horseshit."

Stunned, we listened in silence, and I wondered how Father Blaes, a Jesuit priest could dare be an accomplice to child persecution. Aunt Mary just rocked in silence. Dad held up the octopus thing and continued.

"This is what we call 'The Instrument'. And this here is the board of punishments."

Dad held up a clipboard that had lines and little boxes drawn upon it. Each of our names was listed: Mark, John, Matthew, Monica and Marguerite. Attached to the clipboard was a long string with a pencil hanging at the end.

"Mary and I are going to write down the things that we feel deserve punishment. Every time someone doesn't do the dishes, for instance, he or she will get a check right here next to his or her name on the line that reads "didn't do the dishes." If one of you gets caught with their damn shoes wearin' another hole in the Goddamn couch, you'll get a check right here. There's a line here that reads: "No fighting in the house," and if you do, you'll get a check. If you wake up the whole house with your screamin' and carryin' on in the morning before the paper route, you'll get a check. We'll add others as need be. And then every week or two, I'll line you up and you'll get a hack from the Instrument for every checkmark next to your name."

Dad gave the "Instrument" a crack of his wrist, snapping it in the air. We all blinked in shock. He couldn't possibly be serious. I mean sure, we were high-spirited kids, full of life and noise, but c'mon, Dad was a softy. His preferred method of punishment was verbal and he was so wise and quick with his words that whatever he said made you think hard, which was painful enough. I couldn't imagine him physically whipping us. He only laid a hand on me twice in my life, and both times I deserved it. Well, kinda. The first time, one day back when we lived in Chehalis, he told me to clean my room. I said: "Make me." He did. The second time, we were on a busy four-lane freeway driving back from visiting Grandma Gonder and our relatives in Spokane, and Mark kept poking me in the back seat of the car. I got so annoyed that I told him if he didn't quit, I'd throw his brand new shoes out the window. He kept on poking me, so true to my word, I grabbed one of his shoes and tossed it out the window. Mark instantly blabbed to Dad, at the wheel.

"Dad, Matt threw my new shoe out the window."

"WHAT?"

"Matt threw my shoe out the window."

"JE-SUS CHRIST!"

Dad pulled the car over onto the shoulder, jumped out of his seat, opened the back door and beat my butt. Once we drove off a few miles down the road, Dad said to Mark:

"Mark, you still got that other shoe?"

Mark, the weenie, answered timidly.

"Yeah."

"GIMME that sonofabitch!"

Mark passed it to Dad in the drivers' seat. Dad grabbed the shoe, rolled down his window and chucked it out. Years later, when we were able to laugh at the story, I asked him why he spanked me when it was Mark's fault for annoying me. Dad said my butt would heal but there was no way he could turn around on the freeway to recuperate that damn shoe that cost money. I still think Mark deserves a spanking to this day, but that's another issue.

Nope, back there in Portland in front of a Christmas tree, I couldn't fathom my Dad whipping us. No way. However, if he did, it was apparent that none of us could find refuge behind the nearest priest, as Father Blaes, that same pious man who walked and prayed for hours everyday, was the culprit who designed and created our new instrument of torture. That's why he asked all those detailed questions when he arrived. Talk about an answer to Dad's prayers!

Dad nailed the clipboard on the wall in the living room and the "Instrument" right next to it as a constant reminder for us to behave. These two new objects clashed horribly with the holiday decorations, but when the song "Santa Claus is Comin' To Town" played on Aunt Mary's stereo, and it often did, I found new meaning in the lyrics "You better watch out!"

Father Blaes stayed a few more days with us, during which time it seemed that we got checkmarks on the punishment board constantly. Aunt Mary, in her floppy slippers, shuffled by in a huff and gave us marks for making too much noise while she was sleeping. Later that same day, Marguerite got a checkmark for leaving the door to the back porch open. John wrestled with Mark on the couch, knocking over the coffee table so they both got marks. We thought we were good kids just like any others. That damn punishment board proved the contrary and if anyone were to come into our living room and see it hanging on the wall, they'd run for cover to hide from the young demons that possessed that house. That Saturday, I procrastinated when it was my turn to do the dishes, so I just left them entirely as I tried to pay someone else to do them, and when Dad came home to find a sink full of dirty dishes, he got angry and I got a mark. And those damn marks just kept on coming. It was amazing how many marks lined up on that stupid clipboard next to each name. It was so weird, because we didn't think there was anything abnormal or extreme about our behavior. Why did everyone else?

On Sunday, Monica and I were up early watching cartoons and got into a fight over who got to sit in Dad's rocker, facing the TV set. We couldn't come to terms, so we both squished ourselves into the rocker and writhed about kicking each other until we accidentally broke the arm off his chair. Later, when Dad came downstairs, he flew into a fit of rage, rushed to the clipboard and hastily scribbled on a new line item: "NO ONE WILL SHIT IN DAD'S CHAIR." He gave Monica and I each a mark before storming out to the bathroom to sit on the throne. Apparently he had something else on his mind when the anger took over. We approached the board to see what he had written and giggled to ourselves at his Freudian slip. When Mark, John and Marguerite later read the new line item on the board, we quietly joked amongst ourselves, certain that none of us could possibly earn a checkmark for 'shitting' in Dad's chair. We knew he meant to write "No one will SIT in Dad's chair," but we left it as he wrote it.

Before Father Blaes departed that Sunday evening, he drilled some bolts into the side of Dads' rocker to secure the arm back on. He blessed us in Latin before he left the house smiling, but those damn checkmarks remained on the punishment board. No, not even Father Blaes in all his sainthood was capable of absolving us of those sins.

8. MEN IN WHITE

Dad's prayers may have been answered over the weekend thanks to Father Blaes, but Monday morning brought the answer to mine. The temperature began to drop, blowing a cold wave inland from the ocean. Snow began to fall during the wee hours of the morning, and guess who woke me up crying wolf to get me to help on the route. When Mark shook me and announced what I had been dreaming of, I didn't buy his line at first until John opened the window, made a ball from the piled up snow on the sill and threw it at me in bed. I flew to the window and looked out in wonder. Every branch on the cherry trees was completely covered in a thick layer of soft, beautiful white. The snow had blanketed the roof over the back porch just below our bedroom windows, offering a pristine vision of our whole back yard concealed under a white sheath. In fact, everything everywhere had been magically repainted in a coat of white. Large snowflakes were gently dropping from the light grey sky, and fortunately they weren't instantly melting away. Once I caught a glimpse of it I couldn't wait to fold and rubber band those damn newspapers, stuff my poncho and get outside.

I was in Heaven. There was a good two inches on the ground everywhere, and since it was so early, no cars had yet driven down our street turning the snow on the road into slush. Everything was calm and smelled so pure. Mark, John and I ran out and sauntered along in opposite directions. It was such a treat to forge my own path in the freshly fallen powder, listening to the crunch of my boots as I ambled onward, to then turn around and see the boot marks trailing behind me. I danced and skidded about as I meandered along. I glided down to Greeley and turned right, skating on the sidewalk up to the green house. The grumpy man who lived there was watching me through his kitchen window and stood up as I approached his gate. He met me at the front door. I suddenly realized that I had been taking my sweet time having a blast that I arrived a few minutes after six, and was certain he was going to yell at me. But he was so surprised to see me and pleased to get his paper that he stood there shaking my gloved hand and thanking me profusely for being such a good boy.

I couldn't believe it. I guess the snow put him in a good mood. I went on my merry way, tossing snowballs at street signs as I emptied my poncho one paper at a time. I eventually hooked up with Mark on Omaha Street, where we finished the block together, finally arriving at Mr. Johnson's house. Mr. Johnson opened the door with a huge grin on his face, beckoning us both inside where his wife had prepared hot chocolate and cookies to warm us up. He was full of admiration for our tenacity and wanted to show it. Naturally he made us laugh as he gave us Act Two of his comedy routine. This time he complained that all the stories in the paper were going to be about the snow and he didn't want to pay for a paper full of repetitious blah blah. We laughed along with him as his wife refilled our cups, telling us not to listen to her husband. We thanked them for their hospitality and the hot chocolate that really hit the spot, said goodbye and left.

We scurried back home once we had finished all the deliveries to get ready for school, but just as we turned onto Emerson and headed for our house, John was hiding behind a car, and bombarded Mark and I with snowballs. We aimed and shot snowballs at each other's heads and laughed ourselves silly, until Dad, on his way to work, came out of the house and caught us in the midst of our battle. He laughed, tossed us a couple snowballs himself and then gave us an order.

"Hey, you boys want to give me a hand, here?"

We all offered our services immediately.

"Sure, Dad, what?"

"Why don't you brush off my car for me so I can get outa here faster."

We swiped the snow away from the windshields with our sleeves, making more snowballs to chuck at each other. We were done in a jiffy.

"Okay, that's enough now, boys. I appreciate it. You're already going to be late for school as it is. The girls left a half hour ago, so hurry up, now. I'll see ya later."

"Okay, Dad. See ya tonight."

He drove off and we ran inside to change into our uniforms as fast as we could. We yelled goodbye to Aunt Mary, who sat rocking in her nurse's uniform, and ran to the door until she stopped me in my tracks.

"Matt, wait a minute. Aren't you forgetting something?"

I gave Aunt Mary a kiss on the cheek.

"That's nice, honey, but aren't you supposed to bring something in for the food drive today?"

I had totally forgotten, as I was suffering from snow on the brain.

"Oh yeah."

"Moni' took a can of corn. Go get something for yourself," She said

"Okay, and thanks for reminding me."

I turned to Mark and John.

"You guys wait for me, okay? It'll only take a minute."

"We'll be outside. C'mon Mark," John promised.

They exited outdoors while I ran to the pantry, pulling open the cupboard. I dug around, remembering I needed to bring something canned. At that point I didn't care about the poor, I just wanted to get back out into the snow. I saw an old can of garbanzo beans with a torn label hiding behind the macaroni 'n cheese boxes and had no idea what they were. That can had been there for as long as I could remember, and nobody ever touched it. Anyway, Dad said to take something we didn't need, so I reckoned the poor could figure out what garbanzo beans were used for. I stuffed the can into my bag and headed to the front door.

"Aren't you gonna be late for work, Aunt Mary?"

"I better NOT be. I'm waiting for that damn repairman to show up first."

"Okay, have a good day," I said, and ran outside to join Mark and John.

By that time, many cars had driven down our street, turning the snow into dirty grey slush that splashed onto the curb. Daily life had begun, transfiguring the quiet white dawn into a bustling Monday morning. As we walked the ten blocks to school, we passed folks who were sweeping or scraping the snow off their cars while their engines idled themselves awake in the streets. Others were out shoveling pathways from their doors down the sidewalks, piling up our white treasure onto the edge of the lawns, thus making it more convenient for us to roll into balls.

We arrived late at school, but Sister Raphael knew why and didn't ask questions. She just smiled and told us to leave our wet boots in the line-up along the wall to dry near the radiators with everyone else's. I looked around and discovered all my classmates sitting at their desks in their stocking feet and thought how fun to spend the whole day at school in our socks. John and I hung up our coats and then I rather blatantly placed my can of garbanzo beans into the now overflowing Food Drive box, making sure that everyone noticed what a kind human being I was.

Meanwhile, on the home front, the repairman was frantically installing the washing machine parts as fast as he possibly could, while Aunt Mary hovered about pacing as she continually glanced at her wristwatch, resembling nurse Ratched with a high-pitched Irish accent.

"You better not be making me late for surgery, man," she snarled.

"I'm almost finished, here, ma'am."

"I should hope so. You've been down there for thirty-two minutes already and I have to catch my bus on the hour. There are LIVES WORTH SAVING at the hospital."

She kept pacing. He finally pulled his head out from behind the washer.

"That oughta do it. I'll just run a quick cycle to make sure."

Aunt Mary lost her patience.

"I haven't got TIME for you to be running a quick cycle. Either you fixed it or you didn't, so which is it?"

"I replaced the parts, ma'am, that's all I can say."

She went for the attack.

"Well, if your exploratory diagnosis last week was SOUND, then you've changed the parts that needed to be changed, so now just put the machine back in place and be on your merry way, please."

"I just want to be sure she's in running order, ma'am."

"It had BETTER be. If there's a problem, heaven help me, I'll call you!" she snapped.

He said nothing, knowing he couldn't win. He pushed the machine back into position, plugged it into the socket and gathered his tools. Aunt Mary quickly rushed him through the living room to the front door.

"Ma'am, you don't have to worry. I'm good at what I do, and my work is guaranteed."

She just wanted him to leave.

"Wonderful. Glad to hear it. Send me the bill. I'll pay you for replacement parts, three hours labor and not a penny more and that bill had better itemize everything, you hear me? Now goodbye."

She opened the front door. He just couldn't leave well enough alone.

"I'm sorry you're so angry, ma'am, but I'd like you to know that I'm not taking you for a ride here."

She didn't believe him but could have cared less as she pushed him out the door.

"May God bless you for that. See you in the soup, buddy!"

And on that final word, she slammed the door shut.

Snow continued to fall intermittently throughout the day. I sat at my desk, but couldn't concentrate on the lessons. Very few of us could keep ourselves from gazing out the bay window and daydreaming or counting the flakes as they fell. When recess time arrived, Sister Raphael empathized and let us play outside longer than usual, hoping we'd burn off some of our excitement. When we returned to class, she turned off the lights and showed us a couple of short films on flowers and insects to aim our attention at the wall opposite the winter scene now concealed behind dark curtains.

When school finally let out, the snow flurries had ceased. Sister Raphael recruited some of the boys, including Mark and John, to shovel the sidewalks outside the school, and also the church and convent one block away. I hooked up with Monica and Marguerite outside their classrooms to walk them home. They were both carrying long garlands of colored paper Christmas decorations their teachers had them make to focus their snow-drifting attention onto manual crafts. They asked me to help carry their paper art, which proved to be a difficult task to keep them from brushing against the wet ground. We strolled along but stopped a few times so my sisters could make snow angels in the lawns along the way. Once we got home, Monica and Marguerite strung and taped up their garlands wall to wall in an askew pattern across the living room and then we rushed back outside to play in the yard. Unfortunately, there wasn't quite enough snow to make a decent snowman, but when Mark and John finally arrived, there was plenty on the ground for one more sibling snowball fight before Dad drove up and parked his car against the curb, calling us indoors.

That evening, Dad and Aunt Mary both made special efforts to tell the girls how proud they were of their beautiful hand-made decorations. Before dinner, Dad told us all to collect the dirty laundry that had piled up over the past few weeks since the washer conked out on us, and bring it all to the back porch. We ran up to our bedrooms, stripped our beds and pulled every soiled garment we could plow out from under the heaps of junk everywhere, carried it all down and separated the clothes into color-coordinated piles on the kitchen floor. We were so excited to have a working washing machine again that we ran load after load, singing along with Aunt Mary's Christmas music that filled the air. Dad stood at the stove, making ham and cabbage in the roaster pan. Once it was cooked up, Monica didn't want any.

"What's the matter, Monica, aren't you hungry?"

"Yeah, but can I have a peanut butter sandwich instead?"

"Sure, if you want to, honey, but don't you want some ham and cabbage?"

"No, the cabbage smells like dirty socks."

Dad cracked up, remembering Marguerite's bee story.

"Dirty socks, huh? Well, when I finish boiling them up, you can wring 'em out and put them in the dryer for me, how's that sound?"

We all laughed. Throughout the evening, the dryer radiated so much heat that the back porch, usually a cold spot of the house, became warm and inviting, so we left the door open to enjoy the noisy hum of the machines spinning life in their cycles. We all took turns folding the dry laundry into neat stacks on the tables in the kitchen while the evening progressed, then carried the laundry back to our rooms to put away, proud as punch to remake our beds with clean, warm sheets to snuggle in that night.

We awoke the next morning to sadly discover that rain was melting away our snow. At school, I found it easier to delve into the lessons Sister Raphael had prepared, since there was no longer any white distraction falling from the sky. The December calendar hanging in our classroom next to the chalkboard showed that we had only four more days of school until Christmas vacation offered us two weeks of freedom to do whatever we wanted, but all I wanted was more snow. Now that we had been given a taste of it, I couldn't fathom the idea of spending two weeks of vacation in the rain.

That night to entertain ourselves, we foolishly got into a game of Monopoly. That sounds like a relaxing form of diversion for some, but to the Gonder children, it signified war until death. I threw lucky dice and bought up the choice properties I landed on, rapidly developing them with houses and hotels, paid for with the rent money I extorted from my poor siblings who landed on my property. Mark and Monica quickly were wiped out of the game, leaving John, Marguerite and me to battle it out. Naturally, the game ended up in a noisy fight about how cheap and mean I was for making Marguerite pay her rent in full. She landed on one of my hotels, so, true to my greedy blood, I insisted she mortgage everything she owned. Still short of cash, she offered to do my dishes next time it was my turn in exchange for the money she owed me. Since dishes had nothing to do with the game, I refused her negotiation and went for the kill, ousting her completely off the board. She screamed and yelled in her defense but I wouldn't relent. Dad grew tired of hearing us quarrel, so he broke up the game and went to the punishment board to give us marks for fighting in the house. As soon as he had made the checkmarks, he decided it was time to make us pay for our constant bad behavior.

There we stood with our naked backsides all lined up, not knowing what to expect. Dad counted the number of marks we each had on the board to give us the corresponding number of hacks. He began with the girls. Marguerite started to whimper before he even began to lightly brush her behind as if to swat a fly. Monica stoically took her hacks that in reality were no more painful than a light slap. He then gave me seven slightly firmer smacks and then finished off the cycle with one last hack that stung enough to get my attention, but wasn't forceful enough to leave a mark. Dad gave Mark and John a few harder whips since they were older, but no one was bruised or beaten at all. Once that was over, Dad erased our checkmarks and we finished off the evening stretched out on the living room floor watching TV and munching on the Christmas basket while Aunt Mary laboriously sewed up the worn-out couch our shoes had done their destruction number on.

The 'Instrument' stayed with us for a few more months, but quickly lost its potency for threat. It was more of a humiliating ruse to make us think, really, because as I said, Dad wasn't the disciplinarian type. (One other episode does come to mind when Dad gave us the choice as to whether or not we wanted to take our hacks or carry the checkmarks over on credit. Four out of five of us took our hacks like men, but one person chickened out. I won't name names here to protect the guilty party, but it wasn't me, nor my sisters or Mark.)

Throughout the next few days, the weather dropped and climbed like the famous roller coaster ride at Jantzen Beach. Roads froze in some areas creating ice rinks for passersby to enjoy or not, depending on their inclination. My happiness skyrocketed as snow fell endlessly and began to pile up everywhere. Dad had to put his studded snow tires on the Comet, and on the news we heard that Portland hadn't known a cold spell like this since 1949 and 1950. Kids everywhere couldn't have been happier. I had to help with the route every day, and Marguerite and Monica joined us a couple of times, dragging the red wagon along the sidewalk as best they could, but often the wagon wheels got clogged with ice and wouldn't budge. We were late for school almost every day. There was so much snow in the streets that the plows couldn't keep up. Our street was covered and the slush tracks laid by the cars filled in constantly with more falling powder. The best thing though, was to watch the county population rise daily as Snowmen began popping up in front of houses all over the city.

As we excavated treats from the basket beneath the Christmas tree, Dad came home from work that night carrying a beautifully wrapped present in his arms and placed it under the tree. We had fun guessing which one of us it was intended for as he never put a name on a gift, and by the end of the week there were five gifts under the tree, in addition to the little ones we had bought for each other. I had saved up enough money from the route to buy a Kerbanger for Monica and a Skip-ball for Marguerite, and couldn't wait to see their faces, knowing they had coveted those toys they often played with at their friends' houses.

Friday dawned brightly, bringing us to the last day of school before our two-week Christmas vacation was to begin. The main roads had been plowed making our job easier to get through and deliver the papers. Thank God Greeley Avenue was only a couple of blocks away from our house, so that crazy man still got his paper before six and kept his peep shut. At school, Sister Raphael, on a mission to purge the classroom before the year ended, passed out stacks and stacks of corrected tests and graded papers for us to take home. The maps and student artwork she had displayed on the walls or pinned to the bulletin boards had all been removed and the Food Drive sign and box had vanished. She had us wipe down the chalkboards, a few of us went outside to bang the black felt erasers free of their built-up chalk dust, and finally we had to clean out our desks so that when we returned in January, we could welcome 1969 in an 'immaculate' classroom. Sister Amelia gave us an extra long music class to rehearse all the songs scheduled for midnight Mass on Christmas Eve, and instructed us to be sure and wear clean white shirts with our uniforms to look our best to celebrate the birth of Christ. As the school day came to an end, Sister Raphael served up sugar cookies and punch to wish us a merry Christmas before sending us all home.

Matthew Gonder

9. FREEDOM

Saturday, the first day of vacation was here. After we had wrapped up the paper routes and warmed ourselves up back home with Swiss piss and Cream of Wheat, Mark, John and I went outside to find some way to enjoy our first day of freedom. We looked down the street. Snow was piled up everywhere. No matter where you turned there was at least one snowman to every house and often times it was erected next to an entire frozen family of snow people. They literally outnumbered real people in front of the houses. Monica and Marguerite were across the street working with Renata and her sisters, rolling up balls to help them make snowmen in various sizes on their lawn. The neighborhood looked like a ghost town of snowfolk. We'd all done our duty and made our snowmen already so the thought of making more bored us. We walked down to the corner and hooked up with some of our buddies who were also searching for some other way to entertain themselves. One guy, Kerry Walsh, got an idea. We followed him five blocks down Gay Street to Wygant Street and turned right, and about one block later we came to a hill known as Madrona Park, known to us as "The Bluff" that sloped down to the busy four-lane Greeley Avenue. Across Greeley the hill sloped down to the railroad tracks. The entire area was covered in trees, a Garden of Eden laden with untouched snow. We descended the hill, forging a path to the bottom, crossed the railroad tracks and found empty cardboard boxes piled up near a freight stocking building. Kerry told us to get our mitts on a large empty box and flatten it, which we all did, and then carried them back over the tracks to make the slow hike up the hill. At first we didn't have a clue as to what we were doing all of this for, but when you're caught in an adventure, you don't ask questions. Time no longer exists and you just follow the leader. Once we reached the top of the hill, Kerry demonstrated. He laid his flattened box on the snow, hopped on and began sliding down the hill at wind breaking speed. We didn't need coaxing. We all immediately followed suit and spent the afternoon cardboard sledding down The Bluff. Now that was what we called fun. I can't count how many times we avoided trees or crashed into a ditch, nor the times we almost slid into the first lane of busy traffic at the bottom of the hill on Greeley.

We lost track of time but knew we should go home once it began to get dark. We had worn ourselves out from sledding and hiking back up that hill all afternoon and our fingers and toes were frozen, so we dreaded the walk home. Kerry Walsh offered another idea.

"All you gotta do is squat down behind a parked car, and when another car comes driving down the street, you jump out from your hiding place, grab the bumper of the car and slide along as far as you wanna go. It's called Hooky Bobbing."

"You gotta be kiddin' me."

"I'm not. Watch. You guys stand back over there. Don't blow my hidin' place."

Kerry crouched down between two parked cars and waited. We stood away from him on the corner of Delaware Street and watched. Soon enough a car drove by, moving in a steady pace but slow enough for Kerry to slip out and grab onto the bumper without being seen by the driver in the rearview mirror. He dug his heels into the snow and let himself be pulled along for almost an entire block, then let go of his grip and fell off. He jumped up and got out of the road. Boy were we impressed. We ran up to him, full of admiration and cheers. We couldn't wait to each take our own turns at the new sport. Mark, John and I all squatted down between three cars in a row. Kerry hushed the others back onto the sidewalk and watched us, shaking his head. Finally a car came by. As it passed Mark, he slid out and grabbed the bumper, then John followed, staying down low, and finally I came out and grabbed onto the only place left on the bumper, right behind the exhaust pipe. I immediately started to cough and the car slowed down. The weight of three boys on the same small car was too much to pull in snow and ice. The car stalled and came to a stop. The driver opened his door, jumping out and yelling at us.

"Who do you think you are, pulling stunts like that? You could get yourselves killed! Get away from my car."

We excused ourselves as he drove away. Kerry was laughing at us on the curb.

"You idiots can't all jump onto the same car! It's too much weight."

"And you gotta stay away from the exhaust pipes, too," I informed the lot.

Well, I guess you have to get your fingers burned once to really learn anything properly. We all said goodbye to one another and decided to split up to hooky bob ourselves home. Mark and I stayed pretty close to each other and took turns bobbing short distances on a number of cars. After many trial runs, we learned that Ford Mustangs made between 66 and 69 had sharp bumpers that cut into your hands right through the gloves, but that the Volkswagen beetles pre-66 were the best cars for hooky-bobbing, because they had roll bars built onto the back that you could hold on to comfortably.

When we finally arrived home, John was lounging on the porch waiting to tell his tale. After we all split up, he saw an oil truck coming his way down Humbolt Street. He caught what he thought was going to be a short ride, figuring the truck was on it's way to make some delivery stop in the neighborhood. Right he was about that. John rode that truck down Humbolt Street not far from Beach Elementary School, then turned up Denver Avenue, coming to an abrupt stop that made him lose his grip and slide underneath the truck. He stayed put and didn't move as the driver got out of the cabin and turned his attention elsewhere, and then John crept out from under the truck and waited as the driver pulled the hose and filled the oil tank on the side of a house. Once the driver finished his delivery, he jumped back into the cabin and started the engine. John got back into position, gripped the bumper and hooky-bobbed four entire blocks up to Gay and Emerson. Then he let go and walked the last half a block home. John proved to be the all time champion as he hooky-bobbed the longest distance on only one vehicle. We went indoors and told Dad what we had just learned and done. Dad said we were crazy sons-a-bitches but glowed proudly as we recounted our stories.

10. TIGHT SQUEEZES

Sunday morning we awoke to lots of freshly fallen packing snow. We knew the paper route would be difficult but we didn't care, we were on vacation and had all the time we needed. Aunt Mary was awake early and hovered over the stove in her muumuu and slippers, making oatmeal and stirring hot chocolate for breakfast while we folded the newspapers in the living room. We had our ponchos all stuffed and ready to go when Dad came downstairs.

"How's it goin, boys?"

Mark revived the joke.

"It's a little cool."

"It snowed a ton last night," John added.

"Yeah, I see that," Dad answered, looking out the window.

"After the route, John and I gotta serve Mass at Blessed Sacrament, too," I said.

"Ya do, huh?" Dad felt sorry for us.

"Tell ya what, how 'bout I warm up the car and give you boys a hand?

"Really, would ya?" Mark asked.

"Sure I will. Then I'll drop you two off at church. Sound good?"

"Sounds great!"

Aunt Mary heard the conversation from the kitchen and threw in her request.

"Since you'll be drivin', Seamus, I think I'll join you when you take John and Matt to Mass, if you don't mind picking me up on your way."

Dad knew he had been roped into attending Mass with Aunt Mary. I could see by the reaction on his face that it really wasn't what he had planned for his Sunday morning, as he rarely, if ever attended church. Don't get me wrong. He was a very spiritual man, just not a devoted Catholic. He gave in to make his sister happy.

"Okay, Mary, I'll come by and get you after the route."

"And I'll be ready to go," Aunt Mary replied through the kitchen door.

"Dad, I was supposed to wake up the girls to help us," I said.

"Ah, let 'em sleep in," Dad answered.

"Never you mind about the girls. I'll keep an eye on them and then Mark can take over for me when I join you," Aunt Mary added.

Dad shaved and got dressed while we ate breakfast. Then we carried the ponchos out, threw them into the Comet and took off. Aside from the frozen roads that slowed down the drive every once in a while, it was fun to run the route with Dad. We grabbed an armful of papers, enough for one street at a time, which seriously lightened our load, and Dad drove down and met us at the end of the block to pick us up. We delivered the papers to each house, jumped back in the car, grabbed more newspapers for the next block, then jumped out to deliver them while he drove down to wait for us at the next corner. We finished the route in record time. Afterwards, we drove back down Emerson and there was Aunt Mary, standing and waiting in the window, dressed to the nines. As soon as she saw the Comet approaching, she ran out the door and down the stairs, passing Mark on his way inside the house. She hopped in the car next to Dad and we drove off.

Mass went as expected and ended with the usual Communion zombies on parade. Afterwards, John and I hooked up outside with Dad and Aunt Mary to ride home and enjoy the ensuing scene that always took place with her in the car after Mass. Aunt Mary would become antsy and nervous in her front seat, insisting we drive home directly making no stops whatsoever. However, today it snowed during Mass and the last minute Christmas shoppers were all out and about rendering traffic bumper to bumper, so we moved along at a snail's pace. She grumbled her disdain every time Dad had to come to a stop but Dad made the most out of her agony.

"Can't you drive this damn car any faster, Seamus?"

"Nothin' I can do about the snow, Mary."

"How about going another way? Can't you turn off this mess?"

"Take it easy, will you? Relax and enjoy the ride."

That comment just made her more irritable. She fizzled. Dad knew it was coming and smiled as she hit the roof.

"I CAN'T ENJOY THE RIDE IN THIS DAMNDABLE GIRDLE!"

Dad howled wholeheartedly. John and I joined in, laughing in the back seat. Even Aunt Mary finally cracked a smile as she grasped the humor of her predicament but it still wasn't enough to eradicate her discomfort. When Dad finally drove up in front our house to park, he couldn't resist pushing her button once more. He slowly took his sweet time parallel parking the car, making many unnecessary maneuvers at the wheel. Aunt Mary had her door open the whole time with one foot hanging out, ready to abandon ship, but Dad kept the car in motion until she could take no more.

"SEAMUS! Jesus, Mary and Joseph STOP this damn thing!"

She flew out of the car and bolted up the stairs and into the house, leaving the door wide open. We watched her skittle, laughing at how she comically bounced up the stairs. We followed her, taking our time to get into the house, and by the time we entered, she had already ripped off her Sunday best, girdle worst and was back in her muumuu and slippers, scratching her belly and buttocks and moaning sighs of relief.

Dad took time to enjoy a few cups of coffee and a couple cigarettes with Aunt Mary while us kids ate a stack of peanut butter and jelly sandwiches in the kitchen. Then Dad announced he was going food shopping to buy our turkey for Christmas day, asking who wanted to join him. Of course we all jumped in the car and went to the big Safeway with him, happy to split up and run up and down the aisles searching for and collecting the things we needed for our holiday dinner. Aside from the staple foods and frozen pot-pies and TV dinners we gathered to refill our comfort food supply, we filled our shopping cart with bread stuffing, sage, candied yams, marshmallows, pineapple and maraschino cherries for our upside-down cake, canned cranberry sauce, black olives that Mark would put on each finger before eating, fruit salad, whipped cream and the Cheese Whiz we loved to spread into celery sticks. Dad had just placed a fifteen-pound turkey into the shopping cart, when all of a sudden we heard Marguerite yell at the top of her lungs from way down an aisle on the other side of the store.

"DAD, OVER HERE! I FOUND THE SWISS PISS!"

As a matter of fact, everyone heard her. All heads in the store turned to find where the nasty noise was coming from. Mark, John and I hid down one aisle and pretended we'd never seen that filthy-mouthed little girl before in our lives, but Dad spun the wheels on his cart with Monica tagging behind him and rushed to her rescue, chuckling under his breath.

"Okay, okay, just put it in the damn cart."

We made it through the checkout line, and were given dirty looks from everybody, who apparently had no sense of humor. The cashier frowned her disapproval as Dad tried to hide his embarrassment, smiling timidly, offering an excuse.

"Kids. You know."

She didn't. We could have cared less. We carried the bags out to the car and drove home, jingling all the way, and then stocked the contents of the bags in the fridge or into the cupboards in the pantry, tranquilly assured that we had everything we needed to celebrate Christmas.

Matthew Gonder

11. REVELATIONS

Monday, December 23rd was as snowy and cold as the day before. Dad and Aunt Mary had gone to work, and the girls were in bed sleeping. After the route, Mark, John and I split up and hooky-bobbed home, unable to get enough of our new sport. We got caught a few times, as the drivers sometimes felt a lag in power with our weight slowing them down, but for the most part it was easy to hook a ride. Once all three of us made it home, we met up in the kitchen, drank more Swiss piss and then spent that afternoon hooky bobbing to our hearts' content. But when I began to lose the feeling in my frost bitten hands and feet, I decided to go home to warm up. I left Mark and John and as I walked down Emerson towards our house, I could see from four houses down what looked like a box sitting near the front door. I guessed intuitively that the mailman had finally delivered the traditional box of home-baked goodies that Grandma Gonder sent to her ten children and grandchildren every Christmas. I picked up speed, but as I got closer to our house, I could vaguely decipher more details that disproved my theory. There was a strange looking white bulk sitting on top of the box. Curiosity and my lack of patience got the best of me as I ran up the stairs and onto the porch. I looked closely. The white bulk turned out to be a plastic-wrapped turkey sitting on top of a box with no markings from the post office whatsoever. I saw the corner of a printed piece of paper sticking out from under the turkey, pulled it out and fell into a state of shock as I read:

Merry Christmas from Blessed Sacrament Parish

Stunned, I looked around, convinced that the parish volunteers must have made a mistake and delivered this box to the wrong house. I looked at the paper again and sure enough, there was our family name and address, clearly hand-written on the sheet of paper. What? How could they? In total disbelief, I looked across the street at Renata's house. They were really poor but no box was sitting at their doorstep, and there were no boxes on any of the other porches on my street. Then it dawned on me. Oh, my God, they think WE'RE poor! Waves of shame and embarrassment overcame me in a flash. I grabbed the turkey, opened the door and put it on the floor just behind the door inside. Then I looked around to be sure nobody saw what I was doing, grabbed the edge of the heavy box full of food and dragged it indoors, slamming the door behind me. As I peered out the window to make sure once again that no one watched what I did, Monica and Marguerite came downstairs and joined me. I showed them what I'd found on the porch, but it didn't seem to bother either one of them. They were happy to have a second turkey and to know we had two carcasses for Dad to boil up and make his famous turkey noodles that we would swathe in soy sauce. My sisters wanted to put the food away, but I wouldn't let them until I was certain that a terrible mistake hadn't been made. I didn't leave the house for the rest of the day, afraid I might run into someone who knew the secret.

Mark and John eventually came in from the cold, and finally Dad and Aunt Mary came home from work. I showed them the 'gift' I'd found waiting for us. Neither Dad nor Aunt Mary had a problem accepting the food, but I remained confused and needed Dad's advice.

"Dad, are we poor?"

He answered the best way he knew how, sharing wisdom veiled with humor.

"Well, look at it this way, Matt. We ain't got a lot."

"But - we always have enough to eat."

He could tell I was having trouble in my thought process and tried to reassure me.

"Some months are harder than others, but that's what happens on the move out West. Don't worry, we do just fine, Matt."

"But I thought poor people didn't have enough to eat. I mean, look at Renata and her sisters across the street. They have less than we do and they didn't get a box."

Aunt Mary offered her thoughts.

"But Matt, Renata and her family don't belong to the parish."

"But they're poor, aren't they? I mean if we're poor, they REALLY are."

After all the hardships he'd gone through in his life, Dad still had more compassion than anyone I have ever known, and many times quietly gave away everything he had to help someone else out of a bind. He grabbed and tickled me, squealing out the nicknames he made mine, forcing me to laugh away my confusion, and then offered the perfect solution.

"Tell ya what, Matt-sue from Kalamazoo or is it Timbuktu, why don't we run over and offer that turkey to Renata's mom for their Christmas dinner? If the parish made a mistake and gave it to us, it's ours now and we can do whatever we Goddamn well please with it. I mean the church can GIVE it to us if they want, but they sure as hell can't force us to EAT it, right?"

"Right."

"Okay. But do me a favor. Dig through that box of stuff and give them what you want to share. I kinda got a hankering myself to keep that hunk of sharp cheddar cheese I see there, if you don't mind."

"It's yours."

Marguerite and Monica followed as John and I scooted the box to the middle of the kitchen floor. It really was heavy. Together, my sisters and I pulled out the food items one by one and placed them on the table to sift through. Monica put the cheese Dad wanted to keep into the fridge, and when I hit the bottom of the food bank box I was amazed to find -

yep, there it was - that can of garbanzo beans with the torn label that I personally had taken to school. I couldn't believe it. There was so much food distributed from the collections in all our classrooms that it seemed impossible without divine intervention to have that can of beans return home after what could have been a trip around the world. I still had no idea, and I bet that Renata surely wouldn't know what to do with garbanzo beans, so I put the prodigal can back in the cupboard in the pantry where it belonged, on the shelf behind the five-for-a-dollar Kraft macaroni-n-cheese boxes. We kept only a couple of things we had forgotten to buy at the supermarket for ourselves and then filled the box back up to the brim. Mark, John and I carried the box across the street to Renata's house with Monica and Marguerite trailing behind us. Dad carried the turkey. Renata's mom wasn't home from work yet, but Renata and her sisters jumped for joy when we showed them all the food we brought. We carried it into their kitchen and watched as they put it away. We knew we had done the right thing, as their fridge was almost empty and there wasn't much at all in their cupboards. They thanked us over and over again, wishing us a merry Christmas. As we left their house I looked at Dad and suddenly everything was right in the world.

12. BIG BANGS

The next day was Christmas Eve. That night, the whole family got dressed up, girdles and all, piled up in the car and drove to Blessed Sacrament Church to attend Midnight Mass. Sister Amelia was at the door directing her singers up to the choir loft. I climbed to my place in the rafters silently as I had the willies, wondering if someone might blow the secret and mention that we were poor, but luckily, no one said a word. Mass went without a hitch. Sister Amelia said we sang like angels and for once I got to be one of the Communion zombies and stick my tongue out at the altar boys in service. The infant Jesus had been placed in his cradle in the manger and Christmas had come.

After Mass we didn't dawdle because guess who needed to rush back home and into her muumuu. Dad let us open one present but not the one he had bought us. Monica and Marguerite chose to open the gifts I had for them. Monica loved the Kerbanger and began snapping the two resin balls together, making ear-shattering clacking noises. Marguerite put the Skip-ball loop around her ankle and hopped about, swinging the bell on the string and making the walls shake and shudder. Dad vociferously ordained those two toys to be used outdoors and outdoors only. A little while later he deemed it was time for us all to get some shut-eye, but before I shuffled off to bed, Barbra Streisand began to sing "Sleep in Heavenly Peace" on Aunt Mary's stereo. In an effort to hide the tears welling up in my eyes from everyone else, I looked through the window behind the couch out into the starry night as I listened, wondering why Mom was in heaven and not with us.

On Christmas morning, we flew down the stairs and opened the gifts Dad placed under the tree. When we thanked him, he insisted we thank Aunt Mary as well, after all, she chipped in to help Dad buy us each the toy we wanted. We filled the morning with enough noise to make any Grinch go deaf, but Dad and Aunt Mary didn't even once look at the 'Instrument' or give us a single mark on the punishment board. They didn't dare, not on Christmas day. The kitchen smelled like caramel as our traditional pineapple upside-down cake cooled down on the worktable. In the pantry, Dad stuffed the turkey as Aunt Mary prepared the yams with the baked marshmallows while we raised the sound barrier in the living room playing Ker Plunk, Twister, Rock'Em Sock'Em Robots, Hot Wheels, and a host of other games.

That afternoon, Renata's mom came by to thank Dad for his kindness, but he blew it off, saying he had nothing to do with it, blaming the Catholics for once again making a mistake. Before she left, Renata's mom smiled, inviting us all over to her house the next day for a taffy pull and hot cider, which we accepted with thunderous hurrahs.

We sat down to our turkey dinner with all the trimmings just like everyone else, said Grace to thank the Lord for these and all the blessings he bestowed upon us, then chowed down, stuffing ourselves like pigs. We were Gonders after all. At mealtime, the only thing that ever came between a Gonder and a plate was a fork. Nothing had changed in our recent lives, except that now I knew some thought of us as poor. Funny, we rarely see ourselves the way others see us, but I came to realize, that snowy Christmas in Portland 1968, that you can be what others may think of as poor and yet have everything and even more than you could ever possibly need.

*   *   *

ABOUT THE AUTHOR

Matthew Gonder is an actor, singer, dancer, author, composer and playwright who lives in Paris, France with his amazing wife Pamela and Misol, their royal puff, who the unenlightened vulgarly call a cat.

www.matthewgonder.com

18106200R00070